TONGUES AS OF FIRE

Artist's conception of the author, *John C. Shrier*. A crayon drawing by Dan Smith, 1980.

TONGUES AS OF FIRE

John C. Shrier

G.R. WELCH COMPANY, LIMITED

Burlington   **Ontario**

Scripture passages quoted in *Tongues As Of Fire* are from the King James Version of the Bible unless otherwise indicated.

ISBN: 0-919532-68-3

G.R. Welch Company, Limited
960 Gateway
Burlington, Ontario
L7L 5K7   Canada

Printed in Canada

Contents

Foreword by Ron Hembree

Millions of people throughout the world are coming to know experientially the person and work of the Holy Spirit, therefore, any writing related to the ministry and power of this vibrant personality is of significant interest.

Rev. John Shrier has a depth of spiritual knowledge and a breadth of practical experience. The high level of research and powerful thought that he brings to this book are worthy of your time and consideration.

It gives me a great deal of personal pleasure to endorse both the man and his teaching. What makes the book so relevant is the dynamic manner in which the Holy Spirit Himself is manifested in the author's life. As you read, your life will be challenged and redirected.

Robert Johnson

Pastor of Trinity Pentecostal Church in LaSalle, Quebec, and Host of "Ask the Pastor," a popular radio program in Montreal for over fifteen years.

John Shrier, a friend of many years, has something to say to every sincere person whose heart is truly seeking after the deeper things of God. This book, *Tongues as of Fire*, will guide you in truth and reveal how you can live an abundant life in the Spirit, with your heart alive in faith and your tongue on fire with God's Word.

Ralph Rutledge

Pastor of Queensway Cathedral in Toronto, Ontario, and host of the weekly television program, "Revival Hour."

Foreword

It takes five hours to read this book!

The obvious question is "Why should I invest such a significant amount of time to this work?" The answer is simple: *insight.*

John Shrier carefully traces the tongue-speaking
phenomenon from its inception to modern deception about
it. He thoughtfully makes a good case out of the observation
that "tongues" is not a baby of the confusing twentieth century. Rather, the event was commonplace throughout the
surge of Christianity through the centuries.

When I asked one of my Dutch Reformed friends to read
the manuscript and comment, he said, "The book is timely,
well written, forceful and sensitive, and has a thorough
backdrop of Scripture." Well said, my friend.

Perhaps the twentieth-century churches' preoccupation
with the "tongue question" is just a comma in the paragraph
of history, with little lasting meaning except to provide a
pause. Of course we can't know that, except through the
cold light of history. But, whether it is a comma or a complex
sentence, the issue needs to be settled. John Shrier does
much to bring resolution.

There are books I read like wolfing down a meal at
MacDonalds. There are other books I slowly chew like a good
steak. This book is a meal, not a fast hamburger. It needs
chewing and the meat of the message stays with you.

If you want *insight* to a complex reality, if you want to look into the mind of a classic Pentecostal, and if you want a taste of something good, then invest five hours of your time. I think you will like the interest.

Ron Hembree

Chapter 1

In the Last Days

Speaking in tongues is not a modern day phenomenon of the Christian church...the "charismatic movement" has not suddenly discovered some hitherto unknown dimension of the Holy Spirit.

"Pentecostal" fellowship, embracing believers from all points of the globe, has known this experience in all of its glorious reality for *at least* seventy-five years. It began to take root and flourish at the turn of the century; and indeed is a God-given blessing in these last days prior to Christ's soon return: "It shall come to pass in the last days, saith God, I will pour out of my Spirit upon all flesh" (Acts 2:17).

This very personal manifestation and blessed utterance by the Spirit of God has always been present with the church of our Lord Jesus Christ. Chrysostom, one of the prominent forefathers of the church, shares his observations of the expression of speaking in tongues in the opening centuries

1

of the church:

> "Whoever was baptized in apostolic days straitway spoke with tongues; they at once received the Spirit; not that they saw the Spirit for He is invisible, but God's grace bestowed some sensible proof of His energy. It thus made manifest to them that were without that it was the Spirit in the person speaking."

Speaking in an unknown "tongue" or language is simply an outward expression of an inward experience, and according to Dr. Harald Bredesen, Dutch Reformed minister, "Charismatic time bombs are going off in schools and universities all over the country."

It all began on an historical Jewish feast day:

> "And when the day of Pentecost was fully come, they were all with one accord in one place. And suddenly there came a sound from heaven as of a rushing mighty wind, and it filled all the house where they were sitting. And there appeared unto them cloven tongues like as of fire, and it sat upon each of them. And they were all filled with the Holy Ghost, and began to speak with other tongues, as the Spirit gave them utterance" (Acts 2:1-4).

It is a direct fulfillment of prophecy — thus a natural outflow of an inner overflow. Plain and simple, speaking in tongues is the *initial physical evidence* of the baptism of the Holy Ghost promised by our Lord: "For John truly baptized with water; but ye shall be baptized with the Holy Ghost not many days hence" (Acts 1:5).

It is important for believers to understand the significance of this external evidence, because there are numerous inner or spiritual changes to accompany the gift. Speaking in tongues is an effect — not the cause — nor an end in itself! For example, Romans 5:5 reveals how love fills our hearts: "The love of God is shed abroad in our hearts by the Holy Ghost which is given unto us."

Also in Romans 15:13 it speaks of being filled with hope, joy, and peace: "Now the God of hope fill you with all joy and peace in believing, that ye may abound in hope, through the power of the Holy Ghost."

As a young Christian with a Baptist background, my first experience directly related to the baptism of the Holy Spirit was definitely a "Baptism of Love." Yes, I did speak in tongues but that was simply a beautiful expression of the love and joy bubbling within me. I had no previous knowledge of nor conditioning to such practices. In fact, when someone asked me about the baptism of the Holy Spirit the answer was an echo of Acts 19:2: "We have not so much as heard whether there be any Holy Ghost."

Baptism in water by immersion was a common occurrence in our church, and that step of obedience was important to all believers. However, anything relative to the baptism of the Holy Spirit was conspicuous by its absence. Yet there was no denying the inner explosion of love and adoration that swept over my soul that memorable moment, when "speaking in tongues" became a personal and wonderful experience. My parents did not oppose this new dimension of my Christianity. Rather, they praised God for the obvious changes apparent in my life.

Undoubtedly, this was a turning point toward new power for witnessing, new joy in Christ, a new love for God, and a new love for my Bible. A consuming passion for winning others to the Lord motivated me to work diligently in Christian service and to study Scripture.

My love for God and man increased instantly. Jesus taught that the Holy Spirit would enrich us with a personal knowledge of Him and with a strong desire to speak of Him to the world with a passion for truth: "But when the Comforter is come, whom I will send unto you from the Father, even the Spirit of truth, which proceedeth from the Father, he shall testify of me: And ye also shall bear witness, because ye have been with me from the beginning" (John 15:26,27).

The overwhelming sensation of inner blessing burst forth in wave after wave of adoration and praises to God. Truly, Christ is at the center in these moments of ecstasy. *He* is the center of attention and adoration. His living presence is never more real or more precious. Heaven comes down and glory fills the soul. I found a new sensitivity toward things in my life that didn't honour Christ, and at the same time, a new power and strength to battle and triumph over these distasteful habits. No matter how high you fly it's still necessary to land on both feet and walk straight before God and man.

This wondrous miracle was the means by which God brought me into the ministry. External and visible miracles are part of a God-given credential of the church in a doubting and dying world. It wasn't long after the initial experience of speaking in tongues that God revealed to me how He would heal the sick.

As a young Bible College graduate in my first week of preaching services, a crippled man was instantaneously made straight before my eyes. He had been doubled over with crushed discs and severe pain when he responded to the altar call. We laid hands on him (according to Mark 16:18) and suddenly his body responded to divine healing power. The man went through the meeting place walking, leaping, and praising God. For some, maybe a little emotional, but for all present it was a wonderful experience.

There is no doubt in my mind as to the time and the place where God's mighty power was released in my life and ministry. Late at night, with but a few godly men, Jesus baptized me in the Holy Spirit. My tongue was loosed in glorious dimensions of prayer and praise, and my soul was released to glorify the Lord in word and deed. We should be careful never to underestimate the value of the "Baptism of the Spirit" as a force at work within the spirit of man, lifting him

4

into heavenly places, and strengthening him to do good. Jesus taught such a powerful truth when He said: "When he, the Spirit of truth, is come...he shall not speak of himself...He shall glorify me," and "Out of his (our) belly shall flow rivers of living water" (John 16:13,14; John 7:38).

There are those who reject this utterance of the Spirit as a "now" blessing for Christians. They cite the argument that it was required at the beginning of the church age, but is no longer of any value to believers. Why, we must ask, would it not be as significant *now* nearing the end of this age of grace as it was *in the beginning*?

Long after the day of Pentecost, Peter posed the same logic to convince the apostles of God's dealings with the Gentiles: "And as I began to speak, the Holy Ghost fell on them, as on us at the beginning. Then remembered I the word of the Lord, how that he said, John indeed baptized with water; but ye shall be baptized with the Holy Ghost" (Acts 11:15-16).

It is the same today as "in the beginning" and, there are five words that stand out in Scripture that are directly related to the inspired utterance of speaking in tongues. We will consider:

- *Power*
- *Praise*
- *Prophecy*
- *Purpose*
- *Prayer*

Chapter 2
POWER: Power From on High

Jesus made several statements in reference to the baptism of the Holy Spirit. In Luke 24 He said: "Tarry ye in the city of Jerusalem, until ye be endued with power from on high" (Luke 24:49).

To confirm and affirm to His disciples that it was essential that they wait until this promise be fulfilled He said:

> "For John truly baptized with water; but ye shall be baptized with the Holy Ghost not many days hence" (Acts 1:5).
> "Ye shall receive power, after that the Holy Ghost is come upon you: and ye shall be witnesses unto me both in Jerusalem, and in all Judaea, and in Samaria, and unto the uttermost part of the earth" (Acts 1:8).

Faithfully and trustingly they followed the Master's plan, and it resulted in a supernatural move with utterances and languages never learned by the speakers. Indeed, they were speaking as the *Spirit* gave them utterance: "And they were all filled with the Holy Ghost, and began to speak with other tongues, as the Spirit gave them utterance" (Acts 2:4).

Tongues are the outward (or physical) evidence of receiving the baptism of the Holy Spirit. What about the other external evidences mentioned on that day of Pentecost?

"Fire" and "wind" were both recognized by those well versed in the Old Testament writings as symbols of the Spirit at work. Here again they were signs of the Spirit's coming and descending upon seeking believers.

Tongues however, were the *distinct evidence that they had received the Holy Ghost*. Jesus, the exalted federal head of the church, had shed forth that which would be "seen and heard": "Therefore being by the right hand of God exalted, and having received of the Father the promise of the Holy Ghost, he hath shed forth this, which ye now see and hear" (Acts 2:33).

Proof positive of Jesus' living presence in heaven — raised by God the Father and praying for the descent of the Holy Spirit.

The fulfillment of this promise was to be repeated throughout history, and millions would receive this glorious experience. But never again was it necessary for the symbols of "wind" and "fire" to appear as signs of the coming of the Spirit into the world. Jesus kept His promise — the Holy Spirit had been sent to fill men and women with "power from on high."

This is God's power plan. He knows how ineffective, weak and powerless we are to carry out His work on earth. Our Lord knows how little would ever be accomplished if men like Peter were left without the divine energizing of the Holy Spirit:

> "The Greek word from which we get our word 'power' means 'ability to do.' It means

7

the dynamic ability to be able to do what you are given to do. You will receive ability to do. It will come on you.

"Whatever you do in the name of God, He gives you the ability to be victorious, to live right, to behold Jesus and to live with heaven in view. It is ability to do. The Spirit came to give us inward moral ability to do right, and inward ability to do God's work."[1]

A statement made by the Reverend John J. Weaver, while dean of Detroit Episcopal Cathedral of St. Paul, spoke clearly of the importance of supernatural power in the twentieth-century church:

> "The problem today is lack of power, spirit. The bones are dry and dead. We need a new strengthening of the spirit. I think the reason we are seeing speaking in tongues today is that the world is so fragmented... and in this fragmentation the Christian needs a fresh indwelling of the Holy Spirit. Ministers from virtually every denomination have received the gift of the Holy Spirit in our Cathedral."

Dr. R.A. Torrey taught that with "the Baptism with the Holy Spirit there is the impartation of power. It is the Spirit of God coming upon the believer, filling his mind with real apprehension of truth, taking possession of his faculties, imparting to him gifts, not otherwise his, but which qualify him for that to which God has called him."[2]

It was only after the endowment from on high in the upper room on the day of Pentecost — the fire, wind, and the speaking in tongues — that thousands responded to Peter's preaching. What did "speaking in tongues" have to do with personal power to preach? The obvious answer is that "tongues" in themselves represented a miracle of faith.

8

Plainly, it says, "as the Spirit gave them utterance." It was and is a miraculous manifestation of the supernatural power of God to the one who experiences such inspired speech, which in turn quickens the preaching of the gospel.

It also made Peter, and all who were with him, aware of a new and powerful presence at work in their lives. Being guided by the Holy Spirit and knowing this was a fulfillment of Joel's prophecy, added a degree of boldness never witnessed in these men before Pentecost. They were not cowed by the crowd, nor intimidated by negative and insulting remarks. There was a bold declaration, preached in the power and demonstration of the Spirit.

This evident token of the moving of the Holy Spirit gripped them so deeply that they could look right into the face of the impossible and challenge the very forces of hell. All hesitation and doubt faded, giving way to faith that could challenge sin and sickness.

"Look on us," they commanded a man who had been lame for forty years. Boldness swept over their spirits, holy authority took charge of the situation, and a hand of faith reached down with the words, "In the name of Jesus of Nazareth rise up and walk...the man walked...leaped... praised God" (Acts 3:4-8).

Apostolic power was released in that upper room, and "speaking in tongues" played an important part in strengthening faith in miracle power for *all* present.

We are experiencing and witnessing this same work today. Dr. Paul Kauffman, outstanding missionary statesman and author, says in his book, *China Tomorrow*: "The divine fire is graciously torching the church in many places and accomplishing more in half a day than ministers and missionaries can in half a lifetime. In answer to earnest prayer for infilling, the Holy Spirit is descending on His church and empowering it to be righteous, do justice, and rejoice in the Lord. A vast dedication of life at all levels is going on in the race-and-culture-transcending household of God, giving promise of new reservoirs of power for the many tasks which God, the righteous judge, assigns to His servants."[3]

Power from on high is a prime requisite if God's assigned tasks are to be *fulfilled*.

Divine energizing for Christian service has never been more necessary than in these last days prior to Christ's return. If this particular power was necessary for the church's original leaders in order to evangelize the world, how much more so now?

What has speaking in tongues to do with these mighty spiritual works? To the one aware of this power a miracle work is revealed, motivating them to believe that all other signs of God's supernatural workings are equally possible in and through His church.

Mark 16:17,18 says:

> "These signs shall follow them that believe; In my name shall they cast out devils; they shall speak with new tongues; They shall take up serpents; and if they drink any deadly thing, it shall not hurt them; they shall lay hands on the sick, and they shall recover."

Listen once again to Dr. Paul Kauffman: "We are witnessing the strengthening and cleansing of the church. Denominational walls are crumbling. Joy of the Lord is returning to the church; praise and worship are in the forefront of the church's new awareness of God's presence. *New* power has come to the church universal as more and more of God's children move in the *power of the Holy Spirit.*"[4]

There are now no boundaries when "speaking in tongues" is mentioned among various church leaders. The charismatic movement is common to all denominations...Roman Catholic as well as Protestant.

Graham Pulkingham, as the pastor of the Episcopal Church of the Redeemer in Houston, provides just one example of what God is doing in our generation. He publicly stated:

> "Rather soon after I knelt, all awareness of

the men and their prayers, of the room, and even of myself was obliterated by the immense presence. He was unmistakably there...In a moment of breathless adoration, all my longing for love was satisfied and my inner being was swept clean of defilement from the tip of my toes to the top of my head as with a mighty rush of wind."[5]

Power, peace, and joyous presence are all exciting, new realities when the Holy Spirit is given His place in our lives.

"Tongues" on the day of Pentecost revealed to this feeble flock that God had truly visited them in answer to the prayer of their Lord. Christ promised them a Comforter from within to help, and He promised that the Father would honor His petition in this crucial beginning of the church:

"And I will pray the Father, and he shall give you another Comforter, that he may abide with you for ever; I will not leave you comfortless: I will come to you. But the Comforter, which is the Holy Ghost, whom the Father will send in my name, he shall teach you all things, and bring all things to your remembrance, whatsoever I have said unto you" (John 14:16,18,26).
"Nevertheless I tell you the truth; It is expedient for you that I go away: for if I go not away, the Comforter will not come unto you; but if I depart, I will send him unto you" (John 16:7).

Confidence burst forth from these new followers, for they knew this explosive divine utterance falling from their lips was a direct answer to prayer. It was also confirmation of what could be expected in the future as God worked with them.

The scriptures tell us, "they went forth, and preached every where, *the Lord working with them*, and confirming the word with signs following" (Mark 16:20).

There are those who mistakenly believe the utterances of the Holy Spirit are to be a form of prophecy...preaching. They claim that this was the case on the day of Pentecost. Peter put that theory to rest when he stood to declare:

> "But this is that which was spoken by the prophet Joel; And it shall come to pass in the last days, saith God, I will pour out of my Spirit upon all flesh: and your sons and your daughters shall prophesy, and your young men shall see visions, and your old men shall dream dreams"
>
> "For the promise is unto you, and to your children, and to all that are afar off, even as many as the Lord our God shall call" (Acts 2:16, 17, 39).

Peter knew he had received the gift of the Spirit, and declared it to be a fulfillment of prophecy. He preached with such power and force that on that one day alone 3,000 souls were won to the Lord. (Acts 9:41.) Peter knew his preaching was God's message to this audience, and he called them to repentance saying "Save yourselves from this untoward generation" (Acts 2:40).

This certainly is in keeping with the Lord's promise to His followers:

> "The Comforter...whom the Father will send in my name, he shall teach you all things, whatsoever I have said unto you" (John 14:26).
>
> "When he, the Spirit of truth, is come, he will guide you into all truth: for he shall not speak of himself; but whatsoever he shall

hear, that shall he speak: and he will shew you things to come" (John 16:13).

The fact that Peter was able to relate this historical happening to the prophetic Word from Joel, made it apparent that the Spirit of God was at work, for it was the Holy Spirit who revealed this truth to him. Peter's complete sermon involved three major applications of Old Testament prophecy:

- Joel 2:28-31
- Psalm 16:8-11
- Psalm 110:1

It is scriptural insight that puts the power into preaching, and it is the Holy Spirit's work to bring truth to light and teach us biblical application in Christian experience.

The Reverend Dennis Bennett, an Anglican priest, has a good word on the importance of the Spirit's work and Scripture:

> "As a Christian baptized in the Holy Spirit, you will find the Bible speaking to you all the way through, even though you do not always understand the background of what you are reading. This is the most important use of the Scriptures, to let the Holy Spirit speak to you...
>
> "Intellectual understanding and training in the faith are important, but the most important ministry of the Bible to you will be inspiration. You need to let God speak to you personally through His Word. The Christian life must be an interplay of experience and truth.
>
> "Anyone making a study of the Pentecostal movement will discover that the devotional life is very important and meaningful for a Pentecostal Christian. The impetus or

motivation for this deeper devotional life
has been due primarily to two factors: the
recognition of the doctrine and ministry of
the Holy Spirit, and the individual believer's
baptism in the Holy Spirit, accompanied by
speaking in other tongues."

This great new-found power certainly embraces the scriptures and leads to high moments of personal inspiration.

W.J. Hollenweger was critical of Pentecostals for holding a
rigid position in regard to the Bible as the inspired Word of
God and the infallible rule of faith and conduct, but he
defends them against critics who accuse them of neglecting
the Bible. He states:

"The critics of the Pentecostal movement
who accuse it of neglecting the written
Word in favor of individual illuminations by
the Spirit, are ignorant of the role which the
Bible plays in the Pentecostal movement.
Pentecostals live with the Bible. They read it
every day and know many passages by
heart. The words of the Bible are woven into their prayers and writings."[6]

It is personal inspiration and insights into Holy Scripture that
are very important elements to all Christians receiving the
baptism of the Holy Spirit. A Christian opening the door and
stepping into a languoring world with these companions has
the provision of kindly helpmates in the journey before him.

Chapter 3

PRAISE: Magnify Him in Your Hearts

Praising God in an unknown tongue is a marvelous release of the soul. When you feel so full of God's presence that you can no longer contain His blessing and joy, suddenly, from deep within flows a new language, allowing you freedom to praise God in the Spirit: "He that believeth on me, as the scripture hath said, out of his belly shall flow rivers of living water" (John 7:38).

The first mention of this particular dimension is recorded in Acts 10:46: "For they heard them speak with tongues, and magnify God."

This took place in the household of the Roman, Cornelius, and the Jewish believers with Peter readily recognized the Gentiles as Christians based on the fact that "they heard them speak with tongues." Peter's explanation at Jerusalem was, "What was I, that I could withstand God?" (Acts 11:17,18.) Receiving the Spirit was the grounds for allowing the "Gentile" Christians to be baptized in water. After witnessing the event of the Holy Spirit falling upon these believers Peter asks, "Can *any man* forbid water, that these should not be baptized, which have received the Holy Ghost as well as we?" (Acts 10:47.)

According to the teaching of St. Paul, in these moments of ecstasy we are speaking not unto men, but unto God: "For he that speaketh in an unknown tongue speaketh not unto men, but unto God: for no man understandeth him; howbeit in the spirit he speaketh mysteries" (I Corinthians 14:2).

Once we have spoken in this heavenly language it becomes a natural and blessed way to respond when the Spirit comes upon you: "I will pray with the spirit, and I will pray with the understanding also: I will sing with the spirit, and I will sing with the understanding also" (I Corinthians 14:15).

Singing "with the Spirit" (I Corinthians 14:15) is always prominent in the teachings of St. Paul. When instructing us to remain filled with the Spirit, or to walk in the Spirit, singing is emphasized as part of this precious process. "Speaking to yourselves in psalms and hymns and spiritual songs, singing and making melody in your heart to the Lord" (Ephesians 5:19).

Anyone having experienced a fluency in "other tongues," clearly understands "spiritual songs" as an expression compatible with singing in tongues.

In Colossians 3:16 Paul again mentions spiritual songs. "Let the word of Christ dwell in you richly in all wisdom; teaching psalms and hymns and spiritual songs, singing with grace in your hearts to the Lord."

Paul stated that he would "sing with the spirit, and I will sing with the understanding also" (I Corinthians 14:15). While writing to the Colossian Christians he distinguishes between singing hymns and psalms by encouraging them to sing "spiritual songs" also. The value and blessing derived from singing to the Lord with knowledge of the scriptures ("the truth") and with the freedom of the Spirit defies description or explanation. The focus, in both the above-mentioned

16

periods of worship in song, is on self-inspiration and self-edification.

Christianity is a glorious religious experience involving our interaction with the Spirit of God. Therefore, Christianity is by nature a singing religion, and singing with the Spirit is very real and significant. Spiritual awakenings have always brought renewed emphasis on singing with joy. John Wesley wrote in a hymn book: "Sing lustily and with courage. Beware of singing as if you were half dead, or half asleep; but lift up your voice with strength."

It develops into an accepted and dynamic expression of praise in singing and worship before the Lord. Paul certainly must have enjoyed this freedom in worship. No wonder he declared, "I thank my God, I speak with tongues more than ye all" (I Corinthians 14:18).

Dr. Robert Frost expressed it very well:

> "There is a releasing power in praise that influences our entire being and carries over into every area of life experience. The Holy Spirit of worship, and the content of the heavenly language is primarily praise during times of devotion. There is a definite releasing power in praise."[1]

R.L. Brandt, district superintendent of the Montana District Assemblies of God, puts this teaching so beautifully:

> "Worship is the hallmark of the Holy Spirit's presence. Where He is present, worship happens. This is true externally. Today there is a revival of true worship that is extremely encouraging...It makes God what He must be — the center of things.
> "Worship is a thing of the Spirit. Apart from the Holy Spirit, worship is mere 'sounding brass and tinkling cymbals' (I Corinthians 13).

"Two elements are necessary to true worship — spirit and truth. 'True worshipers shall worship the Father in spirit and in truth' (John 4:23). Jesus said, they 'must worship Him in spirit and in truth' (John 4:24). They 'shall' and they 'must'! No other way will do.

"Spirit has to do essentially with how we worship, and truth has to do with whom we worship.

"Tongues was a medium of worship. It always is. Worship is the highest exercise of the soul."[2]

Therefore the most spiritual or elevated form of verbal expression is performed *through* us by the Holy Spirit. It is not something that can be manufactured nor imitated by the intellect of man.

The Reverend James Brown, a prominent Presbyterian charismatic, speaks of how the Spirit of God moves in their meetings:

"Our major function is *praise*. We use the Old Testament Psalms as our worship manual, and we do exactly what the Psalms tell us to do. We lift up our hands in the presence of the Lord and we magnify him with our whole heart. We sing a hymn over and over and each time the Spirit of praise gets higher. At the end of singing it in English, we may sing it in the language of angels. (Or as Paul puts it: "tongues of angels" (I Corinthians 13)."

Worship is the creature harmonizing with the Creator. This truth was never more evident than when the initial manifestation of tongues took place on the day of Pentecost. "They spoke in other tongues" — the emphasis here is upon those receiving. "As the Holy Spirit gave them utterance" — the emphasis here is upon the *giver*.

They spoke "the wonderful works of God." The speaking was inspired by the Spirit but was given voice by one hundred and twenty people waiting before God. A word of caution is given here to all who would indicate this as a work of the devil — the Scriptures emphatically say, "*wonderful works of God.*"

There is a real and wonderful power in praise...power to open the windows of heaven, to shut up the gates of hell, and to silence the seducing speech of satan. Praise elevates us into the presence of God and alleviates many a heavy burden in bringing God down to us. That is why the psalmist declared, "Enter into his gates with thanksgiving, and into his courts with praise: be thankful unto him, and bless his name" (Psalm 100:4). David knew full well that the Lord comes to inhabit the praises of His people. Praise can break the dark clouds above your head and allow refreshing showers to descend, and usher you into the warmth of sunshine after rain.

It is refreshing to lift our hearts in praise to God when "the spirit of heaviness" has overtaken us. When we praise the Lord in spite of our circumstances, it is not long before our cold hearts are warmed, our burdens are rolled away and the light of heaven shatters the darkness of night.

In the descriptive words of the prophet Isaiah:

> "For with stammering lips and another tongue will he speak to this people. To whom he said, This is the rest wherewith ye may cause the weary to rest: and this is *the refreshing*" (Isaiah 28:11,12).

Peter picked up on the same truth when he declared: "Repent ye therefore, and be converted, that your sins may be blotted out, when the times of *refreshing* shall come from the presence of the Lord" (Acts 3:19).

Thank God there is power in praise to refresh our entire outlook on life, and to bring fresh breezes into the stuffy atmosphere of our cramped personalities. Lost in God, filled with admiration, and yearning after the object of your love, everything else fades into oblivion. Have you ever enjoyed this refreshing experience? This is the power of praise. Through praise you can be lifted up above the mundane and the ordinary to be carried into the immediate presence of God. As one man has put it, "Worship is a response of our feelings or of our souls, and is therefore a uniting of ourselves with God."

It is a higher realm; it is the "law of the spirit of life in Christ Jesus making us free from the law of sin and death" (Romans 8:2). There is ecstasy "unspeakable and full of glory" as we share experiences of the celestial world. "Holy, Holy, Holy" is the heavenly anthem that sweetly echoes from the temple. Our hearts are united with God's ancient prophet Isaiah: "Holy, holy, holy is the LORD of hosts: the whole earth is full of his glory" (Isaiah 6:1-8).

In the grandeur of such a time of praise and response to our Holy God, there is a deep recognition that our "eyes have seen the king, the LORD of hosts" (Verse 5). Praise and worship elevate the soul and spirit, and make us aware of the High and Holy One who inhabits the heavens. Immediately, the desire for "lips" and "mouth" to be purified to offer the true sacrifice of praise is our consuming passion.

Thank God for the day when His glory dwells within, and we know He has "touched our lips" and the live coals are laid upon our mouth. (Isaiah 6:6,7). Praise flows freely, and inspired utterances adequate for the moment are the words He puts in our mouth. Tongues flowing upward to God from purified lips allows for freedom from the flesh, leading to deeper responses to "the voice of the Lord" (Verse 8).

While speaking in the praise language of "tongues," it has been my experience to feel a release from all inhibitions.

Observe further that the primacy of praise made Isaiah deeply aware of his personal need for a "mouth" and "lips" that would glorify the Lord (Verse 5). Those who exercise "speaking in tongues" during inspirational moments of praise, become fully aware that their spirit expresses their deepest freedom in response to God in exaltation, adoration, and gratitude. Worshiping in Spirit and in truth makes it fully possible for us to hear the clear voice of the Lord calling us to special service according to His will. Isaiah's response was spontaneous: "Also I heard the voice of the Lord, saying,

Whom shall I send, and who will go for us? Then said I, Here am I; send me" (Isaiah 6:8).

On many occasions, while speaking in tongues and praising God, my spirit has softened and become sensitive to the voice of God. He manifests Himself in such precious times of submission and surrender of my faculties in praise. When we lose ourselves in the sweetness of the Lord's presence, there is a spontaneous response to His will.

Praise that moves us into holy harmony with the heavenly hosts always brings honor to the Lord and the sincere longing to serve Him and do His will. The primacy of praise that truly joins with the heavenly hosts, can never be measured except by the burning motivation to harmonize with God's will for men.

How frequent are the mighty, majestic manifestations of God's glory revealed in the midst of praise that recognizes the Holiness of the divine presence! There is that glorious sense of release from earth's plaguing problems and perplexities the moment we glimpse the Lord "sitting upon a throne high and lifted up" (Verse 1). Our soul soars heavenward as earth's menial matters lose their control of our spirit.

In post-apostolic days, historian Philip Schaff reported:

> "The torrent of the new-creating Spirit and life broke through the confines of nature and of everyday speech, and burst forth at first in an act of prayer and self-edification. In an ecstatic elevation, and in new kinds of language corresponding thereto, the disciples praised the wonderful works of divine love. This 'speaking with tongues' therefore concerned primarily only the inspired ones themselves. It was the praise and thanksgiving of their enraptured souls for the gift received...[3]

> "Worship is praise and adoration. It is the articulation of the soul's deepest sentiments,

the uttering forth of love's profoundest thoughts toward its Object. Worship paves the way for evangelism. The order was established at Pentecost. First they worshiped; then they evangelized.

"Paul and Silas followed the same order in the Philippian jail: first they prayed and sang praises; then they evangelized the jailer and his household."[4]

Praise must be kept as a high priority if there is to be power and life-giving preaching in our churches. A few years ago when the Holy Spirit began moving across denominational barriers an article of testimony was published in *Christian Life* Magazine. The story caption was "Church Comes Alive" and gives an account of the Holy Spirit's visit to a Presbyterian church in Jamaica, New York:

"The young pastor at the time, Rev. Paul L. Morris, was a heart-broken minister. The church finances were sour. Bazaars, dances, suppers, bakes, and a vegetable booth kept the mortgage payments on schedule.

"Rev. Morris often scanned Help Wanted columns in the N.Y. Times. But he scanned the New Testament also and found himself asking the question, 'How could the apostles launch the Gospel in a world just as difficult as New York and succeed?'

"Wasn't it because they waited for the Holy Spirit's power? He's the One who made their preaching alive... convicted sinners, worked miracles, made Jesus real to everyone. So late every night this young pastor began pleading with God for help. His prayer was, 'Lord, bring souls from the north and south, the east and west.' One night a group gathered at the manse to pray. Suddenly the Spirit fell! 'It was as if the living room had in that moment become an upper-room and we had entered the very dimensions that the twelve found themselves in on that first Pentecost. We had all been born of the Spirit. Up until that moment,' the young pastor says, 'I had been praying. But now He had come in and was praying through me. All were amazed and comforted; filled with a holy joy and a love for one another.

" 'Scarcely had I gone to bed that night,' relates Morris, 'when from deep within me came words in another tongue, and soon I was speaking fluently in an unknown tongue. It was as if something dumb and in-articulate within me had suddenly been given a voice and with David of old my mouth was praising Him.' "

Worshiping the living God is our prime purpose for life and living. Dr. A.W. Tozer expresses this very well:

"The purpose of God in sending his Son to die and live and be at the right hand of God the Father was that he might restore to us the missing jewel, the jewel of worship, that we might come back and learn to do again that which we were created to do in the first place — worship the Lord in the beauty of holiness, to spend our time in awesome wonder and adoration of God, *feeling and expressing* it...as an act of worship to Almighty God through his Son Jesus Christ."[5]

If Dr. Tozer is right when he said, "Worship is the missing jewel in the evangelical church" we ought to welcome any fresh movings of the Holy Spirit. We are in no position to

23

bargain with God as to how worship is to be expressed. If "speaking in tongues" is part of His plan then we must allow, welcome and even seek such meaningful expressions of praise.

For too long church leaders have felt it their personal responsibility to legislate against miraculous utterances during times of prayer and praise. Praise, according to God's Word, certainly allows for supernatural speech during services of worship.

Dr. J. Daniel Bouman observes:

> "One notable thing about a New Testament church service must have been that almost everyone came feeling he had the privilege of contributing something to it.
> "To sum up, my friends: when you meet for worship each of you contributes a hymn, some instruction, a revelation, an ecstatic utterance or the interpretation of such utterances (I Corinthians 14:26, NEB)."[6]

The moving of the Holy Spirit with "tongues" and the "interpretation of tongues" belongs to Christian worship, and offers the distinct inspirational qualities of "exhortation, edification and comfort."

It is enough that God has called this holy. We need not reject the work of His Spirit as unnecessary or unholy. Paul, concerned that worship might become legalistic, static and formal, warns the church, "Forbid not to speak with tongues" (I Corinthians 14:39). What if speaking in tongues was introduced as God's way of encouraging spontaneity and freshness in our worship? Would it not then be tragic to reject this new wave of spiritual life?

This could be the answer to the question of Christian leaders asking how to rectify the matter of "ministerial monopoly...conducting the service." It seems obvious that worshiping in the Spirit offers a divine provision for the human need of renewal in praise. Remember the lyrics of the old

24

church hymn:

> "O for a thousand tongues to sing
> My great Redeemer's praise.
> The glories of my God and King
> The triumphs of His grace."

The apostle Paul certainly thought it appropriate for *all* believers. "I would that ye all spake with tongues" (I Corinthians 14:5).

Consider the personal comments of Dr. Van Dusen after his visit to his first Pentecostal service in the Caribbean:

> "I felt rather at home," he said. "In spite of the vast differences — and they were certainly vast — I felt at home. I felt that I was stepping back in time to a primitive but very vital Christian experience. I do believe that Peter and Barnabas and Paul would find themselves more at home in a good Pentecostal service than in the formalized and ritualized worship of most of our modern churches."

He came away, too, with an impression about tongues:

> "It seemed too that this 'speaking in tongues' was a kind of spiritual therapy. It was quite unsettling hearing tongues for the first time. But one impression stands out above the rest. I came away feeling that this was an emotional people better off; released, relaxed."

He continued his evaluation indicating that he had not spoken in tongues himself but suggests:

> "This, it seems to me, is what tongues is all

about. The human heart reaches a point where words — the dictionary definition of words — simply aren't adequate to express all that cries out to be said. Herein is one great benefit of tongues in prayer and praise, adoration and worship."[7]

Dr. Robert Frost speaks of "the parallel between the gifts of God's Son and God's Spirit. We make the fascinating discovery that both involve an "inward work" and an "outward expression." The Scriptures declare that, "with the heart man believeth unto righteousness." This is the inward work. Then there is the outward confession or evidence of this inward work for "with the mouth confession is made unto salvation" (Romans 10:10). This is the outward confirmation.

"The same is true in the Gift of God's Spirit in His fullness. First, by faith and with a heart of worship, we appropriate the infilling presence. Then we lift our voices to the control of the Holy Spirit who will direct our confession heavenward in a divinely-given language of praise."[8]

"For they heard them speak with tongues, and magnify God" (Acts 10:46). God's Word is still the bottom line. It is precise and conclusive: "speaking in tongues" does glorify God, and inspires the soul to sing and speak praises unto the Lord Jesus Christ.

Chapter 4

PROPHECY: Your Sons and Daughters Shall Prophesy

The spirit of prophecy and prophetic utterances have a distinct place and purpose in the proclamation of the Gospel. Peter, under a supernatural anointing received in the upper room, instantly preached the Gospel in power. The utterances in "other tongues" had loosed him into a new freedom and boldness in the declaration of God's truth.

It is God's plan that the utterance gifts — tongues, interpretation of tongues, and prophecy — are *all* to be evident in the church.

This is initially expressed in Acts 19:6: "And when Paul had laid his hands upon them, the Holy Ghost came on them; and they spake with tongues, and prophesied."

In this instance tongues and prophecy are linked together. In teaching the Corinthian church, Paul indicates their specific purpose, and how necessary they are in comforting and

27

teaching the congregation:

> "I would that ye all spake with tongues, but rather that ye prophesied: for greater is he that prophesieth than he that speaketh with tongues, *except he interpret*, that *the church* may receive edifying" (I Corinthians 14:5).

It is vital to "rightly divide the word of truth," so let's examine the distinction made between tongues for personal edification, and tongues as a ministry gift in the church.

"The church" is the key phrase that clearly differentiates between *devotional utterances*, and *utterances of declaration*. There are no less than five specific references to manifestations in the church:

- "He that speaketh in an unknown tongue edifieth himself; but he that prophesieth edifieth *the church*" (I Corinthians 14:4).
- "Forasmuch as ye are zealous of spiritual gifts, seek that ye may excel to the edifying of *the church*" (I Corinthians 14:12).
- "Yet in *the church* I had rather speak five words with my understanding, that by my voice I might teach others also, than ten thousand words in an unknown tongue" (I Corinthians 14:19).
- "If therefore *the whole church* be come together into one place, and all speak with tongues, and there come in those that are unlearned, or unbelievers, will they not say that ye are mad?" (I Corinthians 14:23).
- "But if there be no interpreter, let him keep silence *in the church*; and let him speak to himself, and to God" (I Corinthians 14:28).

It is plain that Paul's repeated reference to personal ecstatic expressions are totally separate from what was allowed "in the church." When the differences are recognized, it is possible to clearly understand how one is for personal edification, (I Corinthians 14:14), and the other to the "edification, exhortation and comfort" of God's people (I Corinthians 14:3).

In making this distinction, it is important to understand the place for the "gift of tongues" in the church:

- "Wherefore let him that speaketh in an unknown tongue pray that he may interpret" (I Corinthians 14:13).
- "When ye come together, every one of you hath a psalm, hath a doctrine, hath a tongue, hath a revelation, hath an interpretation. Let all things be done unto edifying" (I Corinthians 14:26).
- "If any man speak in an unknown tongue, let it be by two, or at the most by three, and that by course; and let one interpret. But if there be no interpreter, let him keep silence in the church; and let him speak to himself, and to God" (I Corinthians 14:27,28).

The posture for God's people in His sanctuary is pinpointed in I Corinthians 14:33,40: "For God is not the author of confusion, but of peace, as in all churches of the saints...Let all things be done decently and in order."

An example of this was recorded by a magazine reporter during a service in Reverend James H. Brown's Presbyterian congregation:

"Into silence a woman began to speak in tongues. Her voice was tiny and, but for the depth of the silence, would have been lost. When she finished, the Reverend Brown waited perhaps eight seconds, then with eyes closed he gave this interpretation. 'I shall have a people, saith the Lord, who shall do exploits in the land and be a praise unto my name. The sick shall be made whole, those bound in prison houses of sin shall be set free, for I will yet demonstrate in the land that I am Lord of hosts and the King of kings. So shall signs and wonders be wrought in the earth. I shall be thy courage when thou art afraid, and thou shalt bring glory to my name.' "

God's precious Spirit always speaks of and exalts Christ. "When the Comforter is come," Jesus said, "whom I will send unto you from the Father, even the Spirit of truth, which proceedeth from the Father, *he shall testify of me*" (John 15:26). Further information seemed necessary to reinforce this all-important fact, for Jesus later stated: "For He (the Holy Spirit) shall not speak of himself; but whatsoever He shall hear, that shall he speak and he will shew you things to come" (John 16:13).

Any outpouring of the Spirit, though it blesses us with new utterances of joy, ultimately leads to men prophesying or preaching God's truth. It is plain both from Jesus' teaching and Paul's instructions, that men's hearts and secret sins are exposed before the Lord when the Holy Spirit is at work. "Thus are the secrets of his (man's) heart made manifest" (I Corinthians 14:25). "When he is come, he will reprove the world of sin, and of righteousness, and of judgment" (John 16:8).

Prophecy must be understood to be an outward work of God's Spirit, moving men with a message, and speaking to the lost souls of the world.

Having personally had great fluency in "tongues" during prayer, I have seen a resulting freedom in preaching. Judas and Silas, according to Acts 15:32 (NASB) "encouraged and strengthened the brethren with a lengthy message."

It also appears that *any* outshining of the Spirit greatly influences the effects of preaching. From the day of Pentecost when "there were added unto them about three thousand souls" (Acts 2:41), throughout history unto this very day, the Spirit's work in individuals still leads to fruitful prophecy and evangelism.

In the words of Dr. C.M. Ward:

30

"The Holy Spirit gives utterance. No substitute is ever equal. What the Holy Spirit provides in anointed speech is beyond any lesson in public speaking or any adequacy gained by further education. The best of us need 'utterance.' There is a compulsion that convinces the hearer that God is at work. The 'utterance' fits the occasion."

The results of evangelism under D.L. Moody are described in an 1875 source, *Trials and Triumphs of Faith* by Rev. R. Boyd, an intimate friend of the famous evangelist:

"On the following Sunday night, when I got to the rooms of the YMCA, I found the meeting on fire. The young men were speaking with tongues and *prophesying*. What on earth did it all mean? Only that Moody had been addressing them that afternoon."[1]

Moody spoke in the power of the Spirit, and with prophetic unction to such a degree as to prompt pentecostal manifestation. My point is simply that prophecy, proclamation and preaching are all intertwined with the outpourings of the Holy Spirit. Utterances are given a forceful and powerful anointing when there are accompanying times of prayer in the Spirit. It is all part of revival — our most desperate need today. We need to hear inspired messages, both with tongues and interpretation, and with scriptural instruction often released by the gift of prophecy. It is a positive function that builds up, exhorts, encourages, and comforts.

In the words of Dr. John A. MacKay, in his answers to students of Princeton Theological Seminary: "What we've got to recognize is that many Christians do speak in and have the gift of tongues...One can't escape that many people have it and that it has changed their whole experience. It can contribute redemptively to a *dynamic Christianity*."

Jesus said the same thing in Acts 1:8: "Ye shall receive

power, (dynamite) after that the Holy Ghost is come *upon you*: and *ye shall be* witnesses unto me."

Dr. Robert F. Rice, in summing up this supernatural phenomena in the twentieth century writes: "This present global effusion of the Holy Spirit should bring advances not only *in witness* but also in doctrine and theology. Today's moving of the Spirit upon the troubled waters of our darkening world, is a challenge to every Christian and every local church."[2]

Moses expressed similar sentiments when "there ran a young man, and told Moses, and said, Eldad and Medad do prophesy in the camp." Another young man spoke up and said, "My lord Moses, *forbid them*." His calm response is a challenge to all of us: "Enviest thou for my sake? (are you jealous?) would God that all the *Lord's people* were prophets, and that the Lord would put his spirit upon them!" (Numbers 11:27-29).

Only God knows how important and crucial this need is today. That's why He promised, "in the last days...I will pour out of my Spirit upon all flesh: and your sons and your daughters shall prophesy" (Acts 2:17, Joel 2:28).

We still hear the cry from formalists and liberals, "forbid them," but Paul warned us for all time "Forbid not to speak with tongues" or prophesy as required. "Wherefore, brethren, covet to prophesy, and forbid not to speak with tongues" (I Corinthians 14:39).

When the Spirit moves, men will prophesy to the glory of God, and prophetic power is frequently evident in the preaching of God's word. Not all preaching is prophecy, but all God-ordained prophecy *is* proclamation with the added supernatural revelation of truth given to the assembly.

Dr. Keith Bailey, Home Secretary of The Christian and Missionary Alliance, made the following references to the prophetic nature of the ministry of Dr. A.W. Tozer:

> "The gift of prophecy itself, has not died out. The gift of prophecy is still needed in our midst because it is the anointed ability to

speak to the present need of men's hearts."

He further stated:

> "The more I study revival, the more I am convinced that the gift of prophecy must be exercised among us if there is to be a real and lasting revival in the church."[3]

In reference to such ministries of the Spirit, Jesus encouraged us: "When they deliver you up, do not be anxious how you are to speak or what you are to say; for what you are to say will be given to you in that hour; for it is not you who speak, but the Spirit of your Father speaking through you" (Matthew 10:19-20, RSV).

When the Spirit moves men to speak, we are aware that, "The Lord God hath given me the tongue of the learned, that I should know how to speak a word in season" (Isaiah 50:4).

In the words of Dr. Robert Rice, graduate of Princeton Theological Seminary and Presbyterian missionary to Korea:

> "To evangelize the entire world, is the divine purpose of the Pentecostal movement of this century. *Glossolalia* may be the best known trademark, but evangelism and new life in the Spirit is their continuing goal."[4]

Since Dr. Rice has worked in Korea, it would be significant for us to observe the accuracy of his conclusions regarding evangelism among those associated with "glossolalia." Probably the world's largest congregation and the fastest growing church is in Seoul, Korea. Here are the latest statistics on First Assembly as recorded in *World Pentecost*: "In November, 1979 the 'Full Gospel Central Church' in Seoul, Korea, reached a membership of 100,000. The latest report disclosed 100,930 members and 6,728 home cell units in the city of Seoul. Observers believe the Seoul church is the largest local congregation in the world."[5]

Pastor Younggi Cho expects eight to ten thousand new Spirit-filled converts to Christ each year. All members have received the baptism of the Holy Spirit with the initial evidence of speaking in tongues.

The spirit of prophecy, and of preaching Christ, to my mind, has been the ultimate effect of "glossolalia." Christ became so real to those present in the upper room that declaring Him as Savior and Lord was the natural progression.

If "speaking in tongues" releases us from fear, inhibitions, doubt, weakness and bondage, and brings us into new freedom to declare Jesus as Lord and Baptizer, then the divine plan is fulfilled. No experience in the Holy Spirit should appeal to personal vanity or an end in itself. The all-important criteria must always be, "Does it glorify Christ?" Do people watch and say, "God is *in you* of a truth" and worship God? (I Corinthians 14:25).

Paul's experience at Ephesus (Acts 19:1-6), reveals some very prominent and distinctive features related to the work of the Holy Spirit. This whole event warrants further scrutiny. It is very significant that manifestations of "tongues" and "prophecy" should be recorded with such an obvious emphasis on discipleship and the power of the Holy Spirit.

"Finding certain disciples" indicates that there was a definite search for those Paul could lead into the fullness of the Holy Spirit. He asked questions, he sought responses, he discovered their spiritual needs, and proceeded to minister to them individually. We can't help being impressed with his positive approach and his missionary zeal.

After every effort had been made to instruct these believers, "Paul laid his hands upon them, the Holy Ghost came upon them; and they spake with tongues, and prophesied" (Acts 19:6).

The laying on of hands is one method of exercising faith for the baptism of the Holy Spirit. Ananias ministered to Paul in just such a manner, and "putting his hands on him said, Brother Saul, the Lord, even Jesus...hath sent me, that thou mightest receive thy sight, and be filled with the Holy Ghost"

(Acts 9:17).

When we read that Peter and John were sent down to Samaria for the same purpose (of praying for the infilling of the Holy Spirit), it becomes apparent that this is a divine pattern:

> "When the apostles...at Jerusalem heard that Samaria had received the word of God, they sent unto them Peter and John: Who, when they were come down, prayed for them, that they might receive the Holy Ghost. (For as yet he was fallen upon none of them: only they were baptized in the name of the Lord Jesus.) Then laid they their hands on them, and they received the Holy Ghost" (Acts 8:14-17).

Wycliffe Bible Commentary, speaking of the twelve selected men at Ephesus, states:

> "This does not describe a new Pentecost but *an extension of the Pentecostal experience to include all believers.* No special significance is to be sought in the imposition of Paul's hands for the bestowal of the Spirit. This experience like that of Peter and John in Samaria is designated to illustrate oneness of the church."[6]

One Episcopal minister, who had faced considerable persecution for charismatic involvement told reporters:

> "We receive this Pentecostal experience at the altar rail, by *laying on of hands.* Parishioners from 20 years to 70 years share mutual manifestations of the Holy Spirit in their lives."

Dr. G. Campbell Morgan, in his commentary on "The Acts of the Apostles" clearly states:

> "When he (Paul) met those men he may have felt there was something lacking, something of fire, something of emotion. Paul laid his hands upon them, and they received the Holy Spirit. Then all that Paul missed was immediately manifest. They 'spoke with tongues,' they began to prophesy. Their enkindled emotion expressed itself in ecstatic utterances of praise, for tongues were bestowed, not for edification, but always for adoration. If the tongues witnessed to enkindled emotions, the prophesying witnessed to enlightened intelligence...
>
> "Paul had full knowledge, a fuller experience, he lifted these same twelve men to higher level, until the cold and beautiful accuracy of their honest morality was fused with the passion and fire of the coming of the Holy Spirit."[7]

In our process of analysis we dare not be less honest, nor less satisfied, than our spiritual forefathers. We are now living in the Age of Grace and God has not changed His pattern from when that period first began. There is scope and dimension in the Spirit that beckons all of us to higher and holier ground.

Well-meaning fundamentalists, desiring sometimes to justify their departure from the apostolic position have implied that the absence of "tongues" in Paul's epistle to the Ephesians indicates it was not necessary for this church. However, the Bible indicates the very opposite is true. Paul made every effort possible to introduce this fledgling church to the power and gifts of the Holy Spirit as seen in the book of Acts.

It's baffling to hear profound evangelicals speak freely and positively of the blood of Christ as God's cure for the curse of sin, and then make extravagant efforts to disprove "speaking in tongues" as a God-given evidence related to the baptism of the Holy Spirit. Something that is so obviously recorded as being consistent with God's plan, deserves greater attention. After all, every apostle spoke in tongues and accepted it as a spiritual norm — Paul being the most avid adherent. He was truly evangelistic in his zeal toward the believers at Ephesus, and the pattern was in keeping with previous patterns.

There are three recorded instances where laying hands on believers was exercised in faith for the Spirit's fullness: Acts 8:14; 9:17; 19:6. Three times tongues are specifically mentioned in relation to the outpouring or infilling of the Holy Spirit: Acts 2:4; 10:46; 19:6. A great truth may lie behind this pair of three special events.

An outstanding Bible teacher once told me, "Intrinsic within truth there is a trinity." And in words of Spurgeon, "Grace, like its God delights to be a trinity."[8]

It is the record of holy Scripture we must contend with, not a specific denominational dogma. Is the written account reliable? Is the exposition here strained? Is the approach confined to a limited place, or period of time? Is the manifestation confined to a select group of favored people? If so, why did the brethren in Jerusalem, Ananias, God's chosen servant, and Paul each take definite steps in assuring new converts of their spiritual privilege? "All" present gladly received this message and manifestation of the Holy Spirit. That inclusive word all appears consistently and frequently, when a genuine work of God is being fulfilled.

God's servants everywhere, to this day, continue to practice "laying on of hands" and exercise faith on behalf of believers desiring the fullness of the Spirit.

37

Chapter 5
PURPOSE: Standing the Test of Time

It's often asked of Pentecostals, "What good purpose is served when you speak in tongues?" We have already distinguished between the purposes of devotional utterances and utterances of declaration, but, no doubt a broader blessing is indicated in I Corinthians 14:21,22:

> "In the law it is written, With men of other tongues and other lips will I speak unto this people; and yet for all that will they not hear me, saith the Lord. Wherefore tongues are for a sign, not to them that believe, but to them that believe not: but prophesying serveth not for them that believe not, but for them which believe."

It is another "signpost" the Lord has established to stir the unbeliever, and to strengthen faith in the believer. Tongues, with the interpretation, is a source of edification to the believer, and a supernatural sign to the unbeliever, or one who has not yet believed in this work of the Holy Spirit. The Amplified New Testament translates this: "A supernatural sign to those on the point of believing."

If any would question this mighty reality he must first face experiences of literally millions of believers around the world today. It has been stated that "the man who has an experience is never at the mercy of a man who has an argument." Such a truism would be meaningless if it were not for overpowering emphasis and evidence in Paul's teaching in I Corinthians, Chapter 14. We are never in doubt about this significant sign of the supernatural.

Anthony Palma in his book *The Spirit — God in Action*, wrote:

> "Tongues are not a sign to believers, but to unbelievers. The best commentary on tongues as a sign is in Acts, Chapter 2. The Jews present "understood the languages spoken by the disciples. This was a sign to those unbelievers arresting their attention so that Peter was able to preach to them."[1]

Pentecostals are sometimes apologetic toward the unbelievers present when there is a public utterance in tongues with the interpretation. That is not necessary. Observe the teaching in I Corinthians 14:23-25:

> "If therefore the whole church be come together into one place, and all speak with tongues, and there come in those that are unlearned, or unbelievers, will they not say that ye are mad? But if all prophesy, and there come in one that believeth not, or one unlearned, he is convinced of all, he is judged of all: And thus are the secrets of his heart made manifest; and so falling down on his face he will worship God, and report that God is in you of a truth."

Public utterances in themselves are not always understood

by those present, but with the interpretation comes scriptural orthodoxy and instruction. There is always the awareness of the supernatural presence of God at work.

Rightly understood, we should praise God when He allows these manifestations of His power and presence to occur when unbelievers are present at our services. One meaning of the word manifestation is an "outshining." God allows and inspires these moments to help bring people to the *"truth."*

Author Harold Horton gives a clear and concise explanation related to this utterance of speech prompted by the Holy Spirit:

> "It is a supernatural utterance by the Holy Spirit in languages never learned by the speaker...not understood in the mind of the speaker...seldom understood by the hearer. It has nothing whatsoever to do with linguistic ability. It is a manifestation of the mind of the Spirit of God employing human speech organs."[2]

It is God at work — actively operating by the power and demonstration of the Holy Spirit *through* us. We are simply a channel. There must be a place in our gatherings for all these genuine wonders of the Spirit.

I was thrilled to read a statement by Dr. Ernest Goode during his pastorate of the Presbyterian church in Essex, England. He says:

> "Let critics say what they like...They ought to be very careful what they say, lest they commit the awful unpardonable sin of blasphemy against the Holy Ghost. *The Holy Ghost movement of these last days is of God.* It was started by God! It was empowered by God! It is filled with God! The Word is preached in the power of God. The prayers that are offered are inspired by

God. The joy that lights up all faces is the joy of God. The purity and power that so many receive is the baptism of God. The miracle working power that banishes disease is the work of God. The writer has never been in meetings where so much of the power of God, so much of the joy and so much of the glory is evident...

"I have witnessed scenes, heard testimonies, listened to messages, and shared in outpourings that have almost bewildered me and made me feel like I was dreaming. It was so novel, so unusual, so glorious! It seemed too good to be true and yet there it was before my eyes...

"Here is the real thing that for want of which pulpits are futile, powerless, voiceless, and congregations are languishing and dying."

For the sake of those who might think such positive testimonies could cause Pentecostals to glory in experience only, and to protect against abuses or divisive misunderstandings, it should be emphasized that the Scriptures warn against spiritual pride. "Though I speak with the tongues of men and angels, and have not charity (love), I am become as sounding brass, or a tinkling cymbal" (I Corinthians 13:1). There should never be a feeling of superiority among those who practice any gift of the Spirit. There are no first or second class citizens in God's kingdom.

There is no room for pride of possession on the part of those who speak in tongues. Signs are to follow the preaching of the Word of God, but they are not a badge of spirituality. Jesus had to correct his disciples on this very point in Luke 10:17-20. They gloried in miracles and He warned them to "rejoice because your names are written in heaven" (Luke 10:20). Signs and wonders include tongues but are not for the exaltation of believers above the brethren in Christ.

Paul positively abhorred any expression of spiritual

superiority where tongues were in active use. He taught that tongues as a sign in public service required interpretation to edify the church — not the individual speaking in tongues or the one giving the interpretation.

There is no room for a "freelance" attitude among those the Spirit blesses. Submission to God's chosen leaders is what adds enormous credibility to this expression as a sign to those "on the point of believing." This sign amongst God's people loses its impact when those involved start moving from church to church, putting "their gift" on display.

However, as one Lutheran minister stated, "The cure for abuse is not disuse, but proper use, a disciplined ministry will hold potential abuses in check."

Don't hold back...allow God to work. But keep things in proper order. Paul makes it clear that tongues with inter-pretation cannot be abolished, for if there are no manifesta-tions of tongues for the enrichment of churches today, then we would be at a loss to explain exactly what *is* to be kept in order. Paul said, "Let all things be done" so God can be glorified in the church. The answer is not to see tongues cease, but rather correct abuses.

Some would have us remove tongues and interpretation from public services because of potential problems. In my twenty-five years of pastoral and evangelistic ministry, there has been one dominant feature in various Pentecostal chur-ches — God's blessing was always present to speak to His people. Abuses have always been easy to correct and con-tain where Jesus Christ is Lord. The same Holy Spirit who works supernaturally to bring blessings into our lives, also pro-vides guidance and authority to the leaders when correction is required.

Glorious sign gifts have left their mighty mark upon so many of God's servants. In reading the remarkable story of Dr. Mark Buntain, and his work in Calcutta, India, the testimony of his father, Daniel Newton Buntain, deeply impressed me. The spiritual patterns of this great man's life had already registered with me as a young preacher. Someone said that Dan Buntain had a daily pattern of one hour of prayer and one hour of Bible study. He indicated that this daily practice made it possible for him to always have a fresh message for the people. In following this plan over the years, my life has been equally enriched.

His testimony, in the biography of his son, *Mark*, speaks of:

> "Five young ladies...who were somewhat on the wild side. They attended church, but they were also known to frequently imbibe things of the world...they were not dedicated...careless about spiritual things...worked at the local brewery.
>
> "One Wednesday evening during the regular Methodist Bible study and prayer meeting...these five girls came and began to pray fervently. Before long, tears washed down their faces, and then they suddenly began praying in a language Buntain (their pastor) had never heard before...He knew by the expressions on their faces that something had happened to them. He also saw their dramatically altered lifestyle during the next few days, and he knew that what had happened to them was genuine."[3]

This sign of "languages or tongues" was God's way of taking a man of God, "at the point of believing," into a whole new spiritual realm. From that moment on, Dan Buntain was moved to search his way through the Scriptures, a move that led him into the baptism of the Holy Spirit.

It was to cost him his clerical position in the Methodist church, but the sign of tongues had such a powerful effect upon Pastor Buntain there was no satisfying him until "the power of God struck his life and God filled him with the Holy Spirit, manifested through a glorious unknown language."[4]

D.N. Buntain was to become one of the pioneers in God's plan for Pentecostal outpouring on the nation of Canada.

I would encourage all of those "on the point of believing" to reflect upon and prayerfully consider this and other Pentecostal testimonies. This could very well be God's timing — His call to you — His witness within your heart that this truth has stood the test of time.

Chapter 6

PRAYER: Three Levels of Prayer

Speaking in tongues is a powerful source of expression, and a means of communion with God in prayer. It's that extra dimension so often required during times of intercession. In writing to the Corinthian church, Paul spoke of it as praying "in the Spirit:"

> "For if I pray in an unknown tongue, my spirit prayeth, but my understanding is unfruitful. What is it then? I will pray with the spirit, and I will pray with the understanding also: I will sing with the spirit, and I will sing with the understanding also" (I Corinthians 14:14-15).

Carl Brumback, in his book, *What Meaneth This?*, states: "Prayer in an unknown tongue and prayer with the understanding are both excellent forms of prayer, but they are not one and the same."[1]

There are times when we know there is a scriptural solution to a given situation, and we are able to pray in our language and claim the answer from God. When conditions get beyond the human reach, or human knowledge, tongues become the instrument that makes it possible for us to pray "in the Spirit." This kind of praying is required when human limitations hinder our communication with the Lord.

Praying in unknown tongues by the power of the Holy Spirit is an inspiration to those exercised therein: "He that speaketh in an unknown tongue *speaketh not unto men*, but *unto God*: for no man understandeth him; *howbeit in the spirit he speaketh mysteries*" (I Corinthians 14:2).

Anyone speaking in tongues, speaks unto God, and this has special meaning during times of prayer before the Lord.

The Reverend Dennis Bennett shares his understanding relating to personal experiences in prayer:

> "Speaking in tongues is prayer with or in the Spirit. It is our spirit speaking to God, inspired by the Holy Spirit. It takes place when a Christian believer speaks to God, but instead of speaking in a language that he knows with his intellect, he just speaks, in childlike faith, and trusts God to provide the form of words. The regenerate human's spirit, which is joined to the Holy Spirit, is praying directly to the Father, in Christ, without having to accept the limitations of the intellect."[2]

The Reverend Bennett states the value of praying in tongues:

> "Speaking in tongues enables a person to speak or pray to God without the mind or emotions or will intruding into the picture. The indwelling Spirit says in effect, 'I know what you need to express to God, the Father. Trust me to guide you as you speak.' Thus confession can be made of sins that the mind does not even know about and would

not acknowledge, or would soften and rephrase if it did. On the positive side, love for God can be expressed with a fullness and freedom otherwise impossible to the person because of inhibitions and fears of expression. Intercession can be made for others, expressing their deepest needs, without the intercessor knowing what those needs are."[3]

"I will pray with the spirit and I will pray with the mind also" (I Corinthians 14:15, RSV). The expression "with the mind" certainly does not mean "without inspiration," for to Paul, prayer at all times was to be offered with spiritual unction. "Praying always with all prayer and supplication in the Spirit, and watching thereunto with all perseverance and supplication for all saints" (Ephesians 6:18).

Prayer and glossolalia is not that easy to explain to the uninitiated, but one young Lutheran pastor certainly expressed it clearly:

"It's getting something off your chest, in a way that just praying with your conscious mind can't. When we pray with our conscious mind, only a fraction of our total mind is able to pray. *Praying in tongues* gives the subconscious a chance to express itself, so that one's whole being, one's whole personality can speak to God. When a person doesn't know what to pray for he can *pray in tongues* and grapple with the matter through that prayer, and many times the answer comes to him immediately afterward."

An added word from the young pastor indicated that the Lutherans who were praying in tongues were not people of low intelligence but instead just the opposite — they were highly respected members of the church.

In his book, *The Baptism with the Holy Spirit*, Oral Roberts suggests some pertinent points on prayer in tongues:

> *"For if I pray in an unknown tongue, my spirit prayeth, but my understanding is unfruitful. (I Corinthians 14:14.)* Paul indicates here that when one prays in tongues it is his spirit praying and not just his mind. His intellect relinquishes active control of the speech centers for a moment. Paul insists upon both forms of prayer.
> *"What is it then? I will pray with the spirit* (in tongues), *and I will pray with the understanding also. (I Corinthians 14:15.)*
> "Tongues become the vehicle of the believer's spirit through which he, under the promptings of the Holy Spirit, talks to God in a manner he cannot through his mind or intellect. If one prays through his intellect, his mind creates the speech patterns and words. When one prays through his spirit — his spirit in cooperation with the Holy Spirit — that forms the words of a new language through which the deepest feelings of the inner being are expressed to God."[4]

Praying in an unknown tongue takes us beyond the limits of our intellect and the prophetic promise of Zephaniah 3:9 is fulfilled: "For then will I turn to the people a pure language, that they may all call upon the name of the Lord, to serve him with one consent."

Communication is now in the realm of the supernatural speech spoken unto God alone, and fully understood as our response to Him.

In his book, *The Theology of Prayer*, Professor Wayne R. Spear observes:

> "The possibility of prayer rests not only upon
> the distinctive work of Christ...but also on
> the work of the Holy Spirit...Christians are to
> 'pray at all times, with all prayer and sup-
> plication' (Ephesians 6:18). Obviously,
> prayer cannot be fully understood apart
> from a consideration of the Holy Spirit's
> work."[5]

Paul practiced and taught the significance of three levels of prayer, all requiring the full application of our spiritual faculties.

First, "praying with the understanding" is mentioned. It very simply suggests praying in accordance with scriptural knowledge, and applying these principles in prayer.

Second, there is reference to "praying with the Spirit." Evidently, the apostle refers to praying in tongues. He certain-ly practiced such patterns of prayer for he testified, "I speak in tongues more than ye all." There is no doubt as to the per-sonal application of this spiritual exercise to Paul.

Praying in tongues is the purest form of prayer. As The Reverend Dennis Bennett put it: "It comes not from our still-messed-up souls, but from the Holy Spirit through our spirit, of-fered by our volition and *cooperation.*"[6]

Dr. Robert Frost put it this way: "Paul declares that we are bypassing the limitations of our minds, for in the Spirit we are speaking mysteries (I Corinthians 14:2)."[7]

However, we are "speaking to God" and the prayer is received in heaven. The mental bypass is not a detracting factor, rather an expansion of expression before God other-wise impossible.

The key word here is "cooperation." We do the speaking but the Holy Spirit gives the language. In Acts 2:4 it says, "they spoke with other tongues" but it was "as the Spirit gave them utterance." Summing up the two above mentioned methods of prayer, Oral Roberts stated:

> "There are two ways to pray. One is when

49

the mind in harmony with one's inner being speaks to God; the mind forming the thoughts and words. This often is successful. The mind is sometimes able to reach into the inner depths of our spirit, and sometimes it is not. The other way is through 'tongues.' Your spirit in response to the Holy Spirit seeks out the longings and needs of your inner being and expresses them in a new tongue which flows through your normal speech organs to God. I find that praying in both ways helps me pray more effectively and successfully."[8]

One last element to be considered as a blessing to believers is that they are personally edified and built up in their spiritual lives. "He that speaketh in an unknown tongue edifieth himself; but he that prophesieth edifieth the church" (I Corinthians 14:14).

The third level of prayer, that many have applied to praying in tongues, yet another personal, passionate, pattern of prayer, is truly the intercession of the Spirit: "Likewise the Spirit also helpeth our infirmities for we know not what we should pray for as we ought: but the Spirit itself maketh *intercession for us* with groanings which cannot be uttered" (Romans 8:26).

"Groanings which cannot be uttered" takes us into a realm of intercessory prayer where the Spirit fully controls our faculties. All verbal expressions fail in such crucial periods of prayer. The word here for "groanings" is explained in the Wycliffe Bible Commentary:

> "The Spirit is said to plead or intercede with *sighs too deep for words* (Alaētos). Sometimes we cannot pray because words cannot express the needs we feel. The Spirit's response of sighs too deep for words shows how God through His Spirit enters into

our experiences."[9]

Words fail, tongues seem limited, and the Spirit surges deep within the soul. The Spirit truly makes intercession "according to the will of God" (Romans 8:27).

This certainly isn't a new or novel expression or experience related to times of intercession. In John 11:33 we read Jesus "groaned in the spirit." Also in Verse 38, "Jesus again groaning in himself."

Later, in overwhelming "agony" in the garden of Gethsemane, "he prayed more earnestly: and his sweat was as it were great drops of blood falling to the ground" (Luke 22:44). We are told in Hebrews 5:7 that "in the days of his flesh, when he had offered up prayers and supplications with strong *crying* and *tears* unto him that was able to save him from death, and was heard in that he feared."

So many times in our Christian life we have failed to find adequate words in prayer. We have then identified with Jesus, in "tears" and "groanings" from within and allowed the Holy Spirit to pray through us "according to the will of God" (Romans 8:27). This dimension of prayer may be foreign to some but many believers can relate to it very positively.

Praying is always beneficial, and certainly necessary, so "speaking in tongues" is a desirable dimension in our personal prayer lives. In Jude, Verse 20, we read: "But ye, beloved, building up yourselves on your most holy faith, praying in the Holy Ghost."

"He that speaketh in an unknown tongue edifieth himself" (I Corinthians 14:4). "Edifies" is the translation of the Greek word oikodomēo which literally means to "build up." Here it means to build up oneself spiritually. A related word is used by the apostle Jude when he says: "Building yourselves up on your most holy faith, praying in the Holy Spirit."

To encourage those who desire the baptism of the Holy Spirit, observe the promise of Jesus in Luke 11:9-12:

> "And I say unto you, Ask, and it shall be given you; seek, and ye shall find; knock,

51

and it shall be opened unto you. For everyone that asketh receiveth; and he that seeketh findeth; and to him that knocketh it shall be opened. If a son shall ask bread of any of you that is a father, will he give him a stone? or if he ask a fish, will he for a fish give him a serpent? Or if he shall ask an egg, will he offer him a scorpion?"

Jesus Himself is the mighty Baptizer, and He alone can baptize you with the Holy Spirit. Coming before God in prayer, with a deep longing and hunger for the power of the Spirit, you can expect to be filled with the Spirit's divine presence.

John the Baptist wanted this point made plain when he emphatically declared: "he that cometh after me is *mightier than I...he shall baptize you with the Holy Ghost, and with fire*" (Matthew 3:11). There is no doubt about his intention. He wanted those being baptized in water to know that if they yielded to Jesus, the Lord would indeed baptize them with the Holy Spirit and fire. In fulfillment of John's prophecy Jesus proclaimed to the disciples: "John truly baptized with water; but ye shall be baptized with the Holy Ghost not many days hence" (Acts 1:5).

Prior to the time of his death and resurrection Christ had made the promise personal, saying: "If *any man* thirst, let him come unto me, and drink. He that believeth on me, as the scripture hath said, out of his belly shall flow *rivers of living water*" (John 7:37,38).

The words of Peter provide specific directions in Acts 2:38: "Repent, and be baptized every one of you in the name of Jesus Christ for the remission of sins, and ye shall receive the gift of the Holy Ghost."

Having fully repented of sin, you can then expect to receive the gift of the Holy Spirit as a pledge and promise of God: "For the promise is unto you, and to your children, and to all that are afar off, even as many as the Lord our God shall call" (Acts 2:39).

Footnotes

Chapter 2

1. A.W. Tozer, *When He Is Come*, (Harrisburg, Pensylvania: Christian Publications Inc., 1968), pp. 66, 67.
2. Herman Riffel, *Living, Loving Way*, (Minneapolis, Minnesota: Bethany Fellowship, 1973), pp. 155, 156.
3 Paul Kauffman, *China Tomorrow*, (Hong Kong: Asian Outreach Ltd., 1977), p. 148.
4. *Ibid.*, p. 147.
5. Graham Pulkingham, *Gathered for Power*, (New York: Morehouse Barlow Co., 1972), pp. 75, 76.
6. Paraclete, Summer, 1979, *The Devotional Life*, Richard W. Bishop, pp. 11, 12.

Chapter 3

1. Robert Frost, *Aglow with the Spirit*, (Northridge, California: Voice Publications, 1965), pp. 27, 28.
2. Pentecostal Evangel, September, 1980, *Worship: What it is and What it Does*, R.L. Brandt, p. 10.
3. Pentecostal Evangel, July, 1975, *I Enjoy the Wonderful Privilege of Speaking in Tongues*, Ruth Copeland.
4. Pentecostal Evangel, September, 1980, *Worship: What it is and What it Does*, R.L. Brandt, p. 11.
5. Christianity Today, November, 1980, *Worship: The Missing Jewel*, J. Daniel Baumon, p. 28.
6. *Ibid.*, p. 28.
7. John L. Sherrill, *They Speak With Other Tongues*, (Old Tappan, N.J.: Revell, 1966) pp. 29, 30.
8. Robert Frost, *Aglow with the Spirit*, (Northridge, California: Voice Publications, 1965), p. 41.

Chapter 4

1. Carl Brumback, *What Meaneth This?*, (London, England: Elim Publishing Co., Ltd., 1946), pp. 93, 94.
2. Logos Journal, October, 1971, *Speaking in Tongues Through the Centuries*, Robert F. Rice, p. 44.
3. A.W. Tozer, *I Call It Heresy*, (Harrisburg, Pennsylvania: Christian Publications Inc., 1974), Preface.

4. Logos Journal, October 1971, *Speaking in Tongues Through the Centuries*, Robert F. Rice, p. 43.
5. World Pentecost, January-March, 1980, *News Flash*, Eric Dando, p. 25.
6. Wycliffe Bible Commentary, Ed. Everett Harrison, Charles F. Pfeiffer, (Chicago: Illinois: Moody Press, 1971), p. 454.
7. G. Campbell Morgan, *Acts of the Apostles*, (Old Tappan, N.J.: Revell, 1924), pp. 442-444.
8. Spurgeon's Expository Encyclopedia, Vol. 12, *The Garment of Praise*, (Grand Rapids, Mich.: Baker Book House, 1978), p. 141.

Chapter 5

1. Anthony Palma, *The Spirit — God in Action*, (Springfield, Mo.: Gospel Publishing House, 1974), pp. 95, 96.
2. Harold Horton, *The Gifts of the Spirit*, (London, England: Assemblies of God Publishing House, 1966), p. 150.
3. Ron Hembree, *Mark* (Plainfield, N.J.: Logos, 1979), p. 46.
4. *Ibid.*, p. 51.

Chapter 6

1. Carl Brumback, *What Meaneth This?*, (London, England: Elim Publishing Co., Ltd., 1946), p. 292.
2. Dennis and Rita Bennett, *The Holy Spirit and You: The Text Book of the Charismatic Renewal*, (Plainfield, N.J.: Logos, 1971), p. 60.
3. *Ibid.*, p. 60.
4. Oral Roberts, *The Baptism with the Holy Spirit*, (Tulsa, Oklahoma: Oral Roberts, 1964), p. 22.
5. Wayne R. Spear, *The Theology of Prayer*, (Grand Rapids, Mich.: Baker Book House, 1979), p. 42.
6. Dennis and Rita Bennett, *The Holy Spirit and You: The Text Book of the Charismatic Renewal*, (Plainfield, N.J.: Logos, 1971), p. 60.
7. Robert Frost, *Aglow with the Spirit*, (Northridge, California: Voice Publications, 1965), p. 24.
8. Oral Roberts, *The Baptism with the Holy Spirit*, (Tulsa, Oklahoma: Oral Roberts, 1964), pp. 23, 24.
9. Wycliffe Bible Commentary, Ed. Everett Harrison, Charles F. Pfeiffer, (Chicago, Illinois: Moody Press, 1971), p. 546.